NATURAL MATERIALS

Erica Burt

Illustrated by
Malcolm S. Walker

Rourke Enterprises, Inc.
Vero Beach, FL 32964

Craft Projects

CLAY
FABRICS AND YARNS
NATURAL MATERIALS
PAPER
SCRAP MATERIALS
WOOD

First published in the
United States in 1990 by
Rourke Enterprises, Inc.
Vero Beach, FL 32964

Text © 1990 Rourke Enterprises, Inc.

Library of Congress Cataloging-in-Publication Data

Burt, Erica, 1944-
   Natural materials / by Erica Burt.
    p.   cm. -- (Craft projects)
   Bibliography: p.
   Includes index.
   Summary: Details how to make objects out of such natural materials as pebbles, shells, feathers, twigs, flowers, vegetables, string, and wool.
   ISBN 0-86592-486-4
   1. Nature craft -- Juvenile literature. (1. Nature craft.
2. Handicraft.) I. Title. II. Series.
TT160.B95   1990
745.5 -- dc20   89-32740
                                                      CIP
                                                       AC

© Copyright 1989 Wayland (Publishers) Ltd.
61 Western Road, Hove, East Sussex BN3 1JD, England

Printed in Italy by G.Canale and C.S.p.A., Turin

NATURAL MATERIALS

Contents

Introduction

Here is a list of the equipment you will need to make the projects.

Color
Felt tip pens
Poster paints
Powder color
Enamel paints
Food coloring

Glues
All-purpose glue
Wood glue
Varnish
Masking tape
Sticky-backed
 plastic

**Paper and
 cardboard**
Sheets of white
 paper
Sheets of colored
 paper
Newspaper
Cardboard from
 cereal boxes,
 shoe boxes and
 so on
Cardboard tubes

Whether you live by the sea, in a town or in the countryside, there is a wealth of natural materials around you that you can use to make exciting creations of your own. If you go for a walk in the woods or along a beach or out into the country, keep a sharp lookout. Collect some of the interesting natural objects that you see and bring them home. It is fun to make something that will then remind you of that outing. This book will give you some ideas of what you can make with these collections of stones, pebbles, shells, feathers, twigs, flowers, grasses and seeds. Many natural materials, such as vegetables, fruit, string and wool, you will be able to find at home.

The book is arranged with ideas and projects for each natural material. Once you start to make something, you will have many other good ideas and will want to combine several materials within one creation. Enjoy making discoveries and have fun with the projects.

Hints for working

1. Remember to cover the table top or surface where you are working with newspaper. Maybe you could work on a tray, keeping all your bits and pieces together and keeping any messy work in one area.

2. When using paints or varnish, remember to clean any brushes very thoroughly in water after use. Otherwise the bristles will become hard. You will need white spirit and soap to clean brushes properly.

3. When cutting cardboard with a craft knife, use a metal ruler to cut against. Cut onto a **thick** pad of newspaper to prevent marking a table top.

4. Handle tools and equipment carefully to avoid accidents. Always ask for help if you cannot manage to do something.

5. Read all the directions for a project before starting. You may be able to think of different ways of creating, or decide to use slightly different materials.

Each project will sow the seeds of an idea for something new to make. It is always more fun to design your own creations.

Tools
Fine drill (if available)
Craft knife
Scissors
Stapler
Needle and thread
Safety pins
Pipe cleaners
Toothpicks
Paint brush

You will not need any specialized equipment. The instructions for each project give other suggestions. If, for instance, you do not have enamel paints or varnish, felt tips and glue can be used instead.

Stones and pebbles

You will need

- Pebbles with interesting marks
- Pebbles of an interesting shape
- Glue (or varnish)
- Felt tip pens (or gloss enamel paints)
- Thick paint brush

Of all the natural materials in this book, stones and pebbles conjure up the most exciting and imaginary possibilities and pose the most questions. Where did your stone come from? Has it always been in the place you found it, or was it brought from far away by river or sea? What is it made of? How did its colors and fascinating patterns get there? Why is it that shape and how old is it? It could be millions of years old! To split open a stone means you are the first person to see what is inside.

6

More ideas

Try carving a lump of chalk or soft rock. You will need a pointed, blunt tool suitable for carving, like a teaspoon or thick knitting needle. Look at your piece of chalk from all angles. Does its shape suggest a face or an animal? Has it holes or grooves that you can work on and enlarge? Try fitting together several chalk pebbles to create an interesting form.

Decorated pebbles

1. Wash your stone (this brings out colors and patterns you may not have seen).

2. Turn it around. Look at it from all angles. Maybe the markings suggest a pattern? Perhaps the shape suggests an animal or a scene?

3. Draw and color on the stone using felt tip pens or enamel paints. (Water or poster colors are not suitable.)

4. When complete and dry, cover with a thin coat of glue. This dries as a transparent coat-like varnish.

7

Stones and pebbles

You will need

- Sand
- Soil
- Peat
- Gravel
- Small stones
- Powder color
- Small plastic bags or lidded containers
- Glue
- Thick brown cardboard cut from a large cardboard box, or use a shallow cardboard box, or a shoe box lid

A picture using different soils and stones

You will need to collect different grades of soil (some fine, some coarse). Also small stones and gravel.

1. Select the cardboard you want to use as a base for your picture. Sketch out a scene, portrait or picture onto the card.

2. Decide which areas in your picture are going to be colored. Plan where your small stones and gravel are going to go.

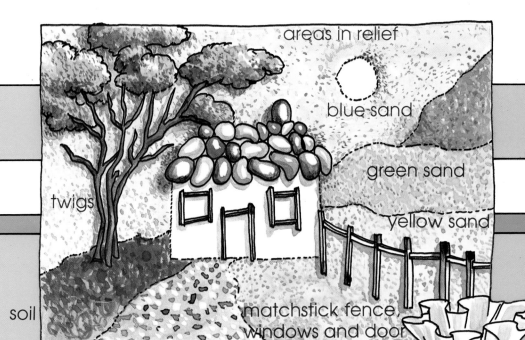

areas in relief

blue sand

green sand

yellow sand

twigs

soil

matchstick fence,
windows and door

gravel path

3. Half fill a plastic bag with sand and powder color. Seal the bag with a rubber band and shake it to mix the powder color with the sand. If you can't find powder color (only some craft shops carry it), you can buy colored sand.

4. Taking an area at a time, apply glue. Then sprinkle the colored sand onto the glue and shake off the surplus.

5. To make areas stand up in relief, mix some soil or sand with the glue separately and apply as thickly as you like.

6. Lastly, glue on gravel and stones. Coating them with glue first will not only make them stick more readily but will also make them look shiny.

More ideas

Add other natural materials to your pictures. Twigs or used matchsticks could make fences or buildings. Grass and small flowers can also be used.

Feathers

Feathers are fascinating. They come in great variety. Look at them closely. There are the soft, down feathers that are light and fluffy, and the larger and finer body and wing feathers, often with delicate markings and colors that only show when you move the feather to catch the light.

You will need a collection of feathers. The best time of year to start a collection is in May and June when birds are molting. You will then be able to find feathers in parks and yards, especially those near a lake or pond, on the clifftops or at any bird sanctuary or zoo that you might visit.

You will need

- All kinds of feathers
- Hard-boiled egg
- Cardboard tube
- Glue
- Pipe cleaners
- Small pieces of cardboard
- Felt tips

1. Sort out your collection of feathers and arrange them according to shape and markings.

2. If you choose to design a bright, colorful creature, paint some of the feathers with felt tip colors.

3. Remember to place and stick feathers in rows from the bottom or end - then they will overlap naturally as in real life.

Make an animal, monster or bird

Body using a hard-boiled egg

1. Stick on small feathers in bands from tail end. Work forward to face, finishing with a band of smaller feathers.

2. Draw on two eyes with felt pen.

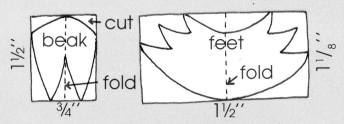

3. Glue on cardboard beak.

4. Cut out feet in cardboard. Glue on base of egg so that your bird can stand. Glue on two or three tail feathers.

Body using cardboard tube

Make up your own monster or imaginary creature using cardboard tubes as a body and head. Pipe cleaners can be used as beaks or jagged spines along its back.

Make your own quill pen.

You will need a turkey or goose quill (ask a butcher) or any wing feather with a strong shaft. You will also need a sharp cutting blade and ink. The ink can be thinned with water.

1. Cut diagonally across the end of the shaft.

2. Trim the cut end to make curves.

3. Cut straight across.

4. Cut a notch.

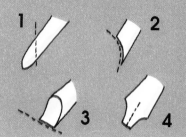

Shells

You will need

- Variety of small different-shaped shells
- Cardboard
- Fine drill
- Glue (or varnish)
- Thread, ribbon
- Paints (gloss enamel)
- Felt tips

Shells, like feathers, come in many forms and shapes. The form of a shell depends on where the sea creature lives - buried in the sand, clinging to a rock, stuck onto seaweed or floating free in a rock pool. Shells have fascinating markings and colorings. Small shells are ideal for making simple jewelry.

Make a necklace

1. Arrange the shells to show their different shapes.

2. Drill a small hole in each shell to enable them to be threaded onto ribbon or thread. If this is too difficult,

More ideas

You can also use shells with different outlines for printing. Take plaster casts and plaster prints of shells. Decorate a box with shells. Make collage animals using shells.

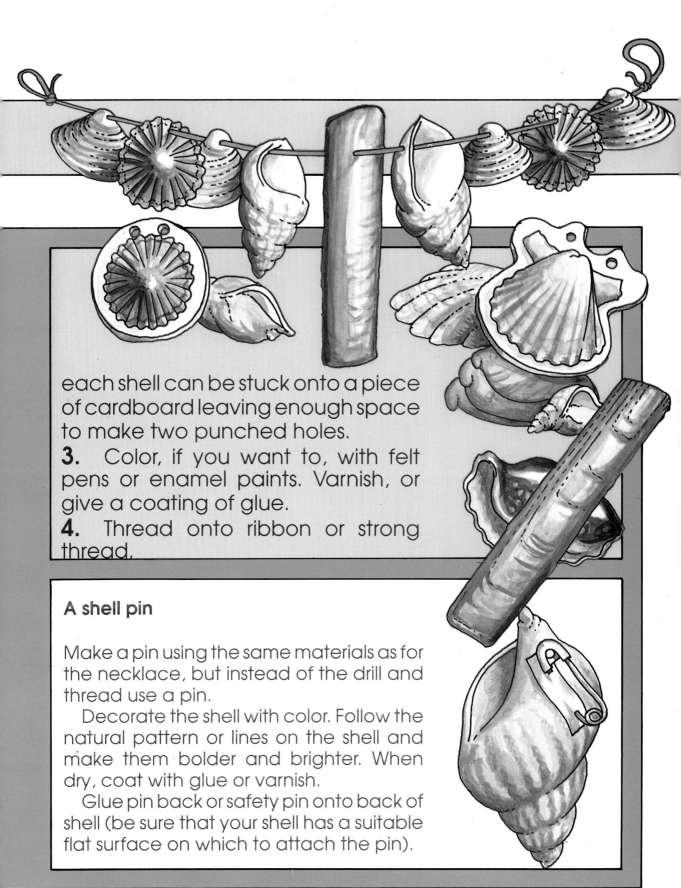

each shell can be stuck onto a piece of cardboard leaving enough space to make two punched holes.

3. Color, if you want to, with felt pens or enamel paints. Varnish, or give a coating of glue.

4. Thread onto ribbon or strong thread.

A shell pin

Make a pin using the same materials as for the necklace, but instead of the drill and thread use a pin.

Decorate the shell with color. Follow the natural pattern or lines on the shell and make them bolder and brighter. When dry, coat with glue or varnish.

Glue pin back or safety pin onto back of shell (be sure that your shell has a suitable flat surface on which to attach the pin).

Driftwood, twigs, bark, cones

You will need

- Block of soft-wood (balsa or pine, or piece of bark)
- Cones, woodshavings, sawdust, small twigs, acorns, sycamore seeds, corks from wine bottles
- Craft knife
- Wood glue
- Sandpaper

The most wonderful shapes and forms, interesting surface textures and patterns are naturally found in wood products. Strange, twisted branches or twigs can suggest a face or an animal and, used together, can create some wonderful images. Strips of bark from fallen trees can be added. Can you find some with lichen attached? Fir cones, acorns, beech nuts and other seeds can be found at various times of the year. Driftwood, collected from the beach, also takes on strange and interesting forms. Think about where it came from and how old it is. Your creations will be even more interesting if you can obtain woodshavings from a lumberyard and sawdust from a pet shop. (The owners will probably let you have a small quantity of wood-shavings or sawdust for nothing.)

Make a face

1. Shape your block of woodbark or driftwood into a face by carving with a craft knife.

2. Smooth off any rough scratchy areas with sandpaper.

3. Put a layer of wood glue over the face area and sprinkle with fine sawdust.

4. Now add features; for example:

nose - long, thin fir cone

eyes - acorns sliced in half length-
     wise (stick on two small raisins
     for pupils)

eyebrows - scales from fir cones
     (or lichen)

ears - shaped pieces of bark or
     cork

mouth - small twigs or sycamore
     seeds

teeth - scales from fir cones or
     beech nuts

hair - curly woodshavings or small
     twigs

More ideas

Make other images with your materials. Be as inventive as you like.

Try carving out features from a block of softwood. Hollow out a mouth or nostrils with a pointed, blunt tool.

Make familiar animals or birds or create mysterious or scary creatures.

Driftwood, twigs, bark, cones

You will need

- Objects such as small pieces of driftwood, twigs, sticks, strips of bark, cane, strips of cork (from cork tiles), twine, string, raffia, sacking, thick grasses, straw, long thin cones, thick waxy leaves, long pine needles
- Thick cardboard (from a box base) 7½'' x 11''
- Scissors
- String and tape

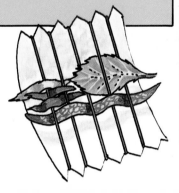

Make a wallhanging

Use your collection of wood products and weave them into an attractive wallhanging. Maybe they are your ``finds'' from one particular outing. This makes a good way to record it.

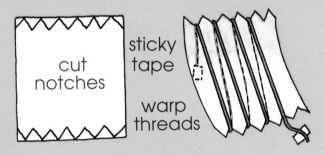

cut notches

sticky tape

warp threads

1. Make a simple loom using the cardboard. Cut notches, top and bottom, ½'' apart.

2. Wind string around and around to form the warp. (You could make a simple wooden frame and wind string around that.) Secure ends with tape.

3. Weave in bands of your different wood products. Several rows of string or raffia above and below a piece of bark will ensure that it stays in place.

4. Knot groups of warp threads together with twine or raffia.

5. Waxy leaves or cones do not have to stretch the whole width of the loom. You can weave string or raffia into the spaces.

6. When complete, turn the loom over and cut the warps halfway down.

7. Group them into threes or fours and knot them firmly at both ends of your weaving.

8. Tie them together into a large knot at the top of your hanging. The bottom tassels can hang free.

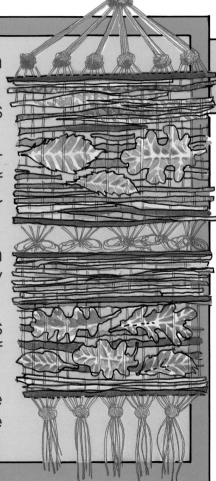

More ideas

Try painting on the inside of a piece of bark. A scene or mask will look good. Collect lots of driftwood and assemble it into a figure, a boat or an interesting shape. Make pine-cone animals and birds as follows:
For an owl, pull off 2 large scales from base of cone. Turn cone upside down. Stick on 2 scales as feet or claws. Glue on 2 more small scales to make ear tufts. Use 2 large raisins for eyes. Glue owl to small branch.

Leaves, grasses, flowers, seeds

You will need

- Leaves (Late summer is a good time to collect.)
- Glue or clear sheet of plastic film with sticky back
- Masking tape (clear tape will dry out) or staples
- Brown waxed paper or brown wrapping paper
- White cardboard
- Round lampshade frame

Coating leaves with glue gives them a protective shiny coating.

Many old crafts use leaves, grasses, flowers and seeds. The Victorians made fancy arrangements of dried flowers and grasses that they displayed under glass domes. They also carefully pressed delicately shaped leaves and brightly colored flowers to make greeting cards. In many countries, grasses, in the form of straw, were made into corn dollies. In Czechoslovakia and the USSR, thin flat sections of straw are used to create simple pictures. Boxes and models are covered with intricate straw patterns very much like a wood veneer. Dried seeds are used the world over to make necklaces and bracelets.

All these natural materials can be found in your backyard, in parks, or in the countryside.

A lampshade from leaves

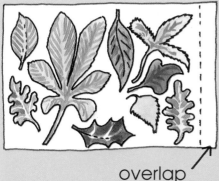

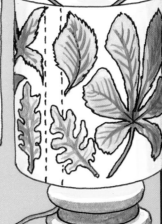

overlap

More ideas

To print with leaves, find leaves with clear attractive vein patterns or an interesting outline. Ferns are very good. Dip into a shallow tray of paint.Place on paper, paint side down.Cover with a sheet of newspaper and press down firmly with fingertips (or use a rolling pin). Continue to print, overlapping shapes and changing color. By printing a few different-shaped leaves, you can make an attractive card.

1. Cut brown paper to a size to fit the wire lampshade frame, remembering to leave an overlap.

2. Arrange leaves in a pleasing way on your piece of paper.

3. Stick them onto paper with glue.

4. Coat the whole sheet and leaves with glue. This preserves the leaves and stops them from drying out and acts as a protective varnish. Or cover with a sheet of sticky clear film. (See pages 22-23 for another way to mount leaves.)

5. If the paper is not stiff enough, attach it to a piece of white cardboard the same size.

6. When completely dry, curve the cardboard into a cylinder to fit the lampshade frame.

7. A strip of masking tape (or staples) will hold the seam together.

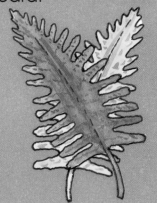

Cut-Straw pictures

You will need

- Straw (from pet shop or garden supplies store)
- Cardboard (7½'' x 3¾'')
- Plain dark-colored fabric (10'' x 5'')
- Scissors
- Glue
- Food coloring or paints
- Small piece of cord or string (3'' long)

Cut-straw pictures

There are more grasses than any other kind of plant life. A walk along a country road or across a meadow will show you what a variety there is.

Cut-straw pictures are a common craft in Czechoslovakia. Straw is the dried hollow stalks of wheat or corn.

1. Cover the cardboard with fabric. Stick edges down on the back neatly with strong glue.

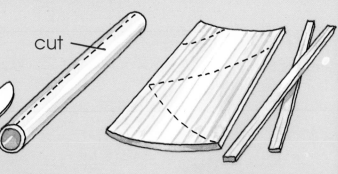

cut

2. Cut the straw along its length. Open out.

3. Cut into simple geometric shapes.

4. Arrange the pieces to make, for example, a boat, a building, a face.

5. Color the straw with felt tips or dip in food coloring if you wish.

6. When you have experimented and found a pleasing design, carefully glue each piece of straw to the fabric-covered cardboard.

7. Glue the cord in a loop on the back of the picture so that you can hang it up.

More ideas

Press a varied selection of grasses into a piece of clay or dough, ½'' thick. Make a hole in the top if you want to hang your tablet up. Without a hole you have an attractive plant stand or paper weight.

Pressed flower cards

You will need

- Collection of small, brightly colored flowers (and fine leaves)
- Cardboard (7½" x 4½")
- Tissue paper
- Colored paper (6½" x 3½")
- Sticky clear plastic film (7½" x 4½")
- Heavy books or flower press

Cards with pressed flowers

1. Place flowers between sheets of tissue paper. Make sure the petals are spread out and that the flower head or stem is not too thick.

tissue paper

2. Put into a flower press or inside a large heavy book. Keep the book firmly shut either by putting it back on the bookshelf, or by weighting it. Leave for several days.

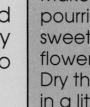

3. Stick the colored paper onto the cardboard.

4. Arrange flowers and leaves on the colored paper. (Do not stick them down with glue.)

5. Cut out the sticky-backed plastic to size of cardboard. Carefully cover cardboard with the plastic to hold the flowers in place.

6. Fold cardboard.

More ideas

Make a pot-pourri. Collect sweet-scented flowers and leaves. Dry them. Put them in a little bag. (You could print the fabric yourself- see pages 26-27.)

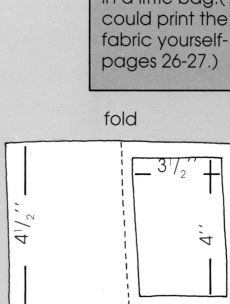

fold

4½''

3½''

4''

7½''

Making seed jewelry

You will need

- The seeds from one melon
- Food coloring
- Linen thread
- Shirring elastic (for a bracelet)
- Medium-sized needle

Seeds of all kinds can be used to make attractive jewelry. Next time you eat melon at home, save the seeds. Wash them and leave them on a paper towel. If you know of any beech trees, collect the glossy, triangular seeds that fall to the ground in the autumn.

Sunflower seeds, split peas, lentils, and other seeds can be bought in health-food stores and supermarkets.

Seed necklace or bracelet

1. Wash the melon seeds and let dry on kitchen paper.
2. If you like, color the seeds with food coloring by soaking them overnight in a shallow pot or small cup.
3. When dry, thread the seeds into a necklace. Use shirring elastic instead of linen thread if you want to make a bracelet.
4. You can use beech nuts in the same way, but they do not need coloring. They are very attractive as they are.

Seed pin

1. Cut the cardboard into the pin shape you want.

2. Arrange a variety of seeds on the cardboard.

3. When satisfied with your design, carefully glue seeds in place.

4. Coat whole design with glue to act as a varnish. When dry, attach safety pin onto back with masking tape. (Or sew a safety pin onto back before you stick on the seeds.)

You will need

- Various seeds - rosehip, sunflower seeds, melon seeds, apple seeds, lentils, split peas
- Thick white cardboard
- Glue or varnish
- Safety pin
- Scissors
- Masking tape (or thread)

More ideas

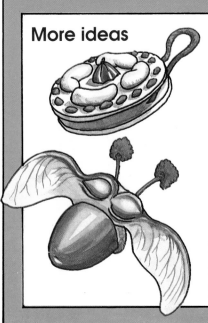

Make identical designs on two pieces of cardboard, stick the two together and spray gold or silver, to make an attractive Christmas tree decoration.

All kinds of seeds can be used to make a picture (as on pages 8-9), together with tea leaves, dried herbs, bread crumbs, crushed egg shells, to give different textures and colors.

Use seed heads, such as acorns or rosehips, and dried leaves to make weird and interesting insects. Sycamore seeds make beautiful veined wings.

Vegetables and fruit

For this project you should be able to find all you need in your home or at a grocery store.

You will need

- Potatoes of various sizes
- Potato peelings
- Raw peas
- 1 carrot
- 2 runner beans
- 1 onion
- Cabbage leaves
- Toothpicks
- Knife

Vegetable people

Use toothpicks to attach each vegetable. Break sticks into pieces when attaching small vegetables, such as peas.

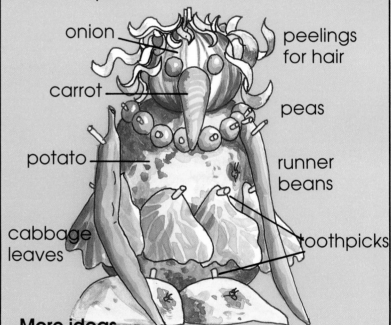

onion

peelings for hair

carrot

peas

potato

runner beans

cabbage leaves

toothpicks

More ideas

Try using other vegetables or fruit: cut tomatoes in half, scoop out the seeds and you have a hat; celery sticks make arms and legs; lettuce leaves make clothes; round slices of cucumber make cuffs or overlap them for clothes. Mushrooms and peppers make imaginary animals.

Fruit and vegetable printing

Fruit and vegetables with firm skin and flesh, when cut into sections, give the most interesting shapes and patterns for printing.

1. Cut vegetables in half, and make sure each surface is flat.

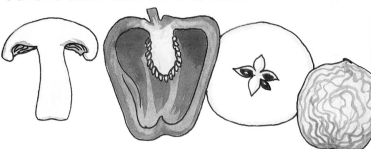

2. Put ink or paint in tray.
3. Dip fruit or vegetable into color.
4. Press vegetable onto paper or fabric to make a print.

5. Print in rows or overlap prints. Use several colors. Alternate vegetables, like the above design.

More ideas

Print a sheet of wrapping paper.
Print onto an old pillowcase.
Print a cushion cover.
Print onto a handkerchief and make it into a pot-pourri bag (see page 23).

String and wool

You will need

- Cardboard (5'' x 5'')
- String
- Glue
- Paper to print on
- Thick paint
- Roller or thick paint brush

String and wool, like fruit and vegetables, can be easily found at home. All the other materials in this book have a definite solid shape - a stone, a leaf, a feather, or shell. But wool and string consist of single, thin lines. It is great fun to discover ways to turn single lines into shapes.

Printing with string

1. Draw a simple outline on your piece of cardboard - it can be a pattern, an animal or landscape.

2. Put glue on the cardboard along the outline, a little at a time.

3. Place string along the glued outline. You may want to knot the string in places to give a varied line.

4. Complete the picture, applying glue and string a small section at a time. Allow to dry.

5. Apply thick paint with a roller. If using a brush, ensure the areas of string are coated evenly.

6. Print your design by placing paper on the string design and pressing evenly over all the design.

7. If you like, overprint with another color, or make a card by using a folded piece of paper.

More ideas

Make a picture using different wools, string, burlap, raffia, or rope. You can create the most wonderful swirling, curving designs. Use string and wool in a piece of weaving. Untreated sheep's wool is very attractive.(See wallhanging project on pages 16-17.)

Notes for parents and teachers

Further reading

FUN-TO-MAKE NATURE CRAFTS
by Robyn Supraner
(Troll, 1981)

SNIPS AND SNAILS AND WALNUT WHALES
by Phyllis Fiarotta
(Workman, 1975)

FOXTAILS, FERNS AND FISH SCALES
by Ada Graham
(Four Winds, 1976)

NATURECRAFT
by Carol Inouye
(Doubleday, 1975)

FLOWERS ARE FOR KEEPING
by Joella Cramblit
and JoAnn Loebel
(Messner, 1979)

Most children love to pick up interesting objects to bring home from an outing. Encouraging creative activity with these finds at home adds a further dimension to simple shell or feather collections and gives an exciting purpose to the next visit to the sea, countryside or park. Handling and observing the natural materials used in the projects in this book teaches children a great deal about them, stimulating their imaginative and creative abilities. For parents, making things from natural materials provides their children with an inexpensive, absorbing activity.

In school there is tremendous value in including natural materials in the curriculum, as it encourages closer observation of the environment and natural world. It is by close observation that children will become interested and involved, will ask questions, expect and formulate answers and widen and enrich their experience.

Each of the natural materials introduced in this book is worthy of much closer scrutiny than the children will give them when creating. A microscope or magnifying lens will reveal much more. Structure and form are explained more fully; a child will see that a feather, for instance, is made up of a shaft that is hollow, and that the vane is not just flat and smooth, but made up of hundreds of small ``branches'' held together by tiny hooks.

Ask children to record what they SEE under a lens in drawing. When magnifying an object, the viewer has to look very closely and carefully in order to record it. Guessing and drawing from memory are eliminated. The children's drawings will become abstract. Particular qualities of the object will be revealed. Discuss how you record the smoothness of a stone; the lightness and delicacy of a feather; the roughness of a piece of bark. As further work is developed, more questions are posed. Which colors suggest the particular qualities best? Which materials and techniques are most suitable to re-create them? For instance, chalks for feather drawings; paper collage for recreating bark patterns; bright, colored ink washes or oil pastels for shiny fruit and vegetables; wax resist for pebble patterns.

Ask children to annotate in single words or phrases what they see through the magnifying glass. This will encourage the beginnings of poetry, or a few lines of description that can be developed into an adventure or story, or themes and ideas that can be pursued in drama.

All the natural materials included in this book can be studied as part of a wider topic, crossing different curricular areas. The table on this page contains suggestions.

Within the curriculum area of mathematics, using natural materials can help explain the concepts of mass, measurements, enlargement, transformation, area, symmetry, sets, number patterns and shapes.

Within the area of science, evolution and change, conservation, soil grading, erosion, flight, aerodynamics, tree and plant life, and marine life can be studied. Natural materials, like fruit and vegetables, can be used in projects on food, coloring and dyes.

Within the curriculum area of language some source of creative work has already been suggested. Children can write from the point of view of the object; such as the life history of a stone, or a day in the life of a shell, or how a piece of wood becomes a sheet of paper. Extend and broaden children's vocabulary with word searches, acrostics and discussion.

Natural Materials	Wider Topics
Stones and Pebbles	Rocks, Soil types Erosion Evolution and decay Volcanoes
Feathers	Birds Flight
Shells	Seashore Homes, habitat
Wood, Twigs, Bark, Cones	Trees Growth Paper
Leaves, Grasses Flowers, Seeds	Plant life Seasons
Vegetables, Fruit	Plant form Harvest
Wool, String	Sheep How wool is made